1981

SIGN LANGUAGE for everyone

BY:

JEANNE HUFFMAN · BOBBI HOFFMAN · DAVID GRANSEE
ANNE FOX · JUANITA JAMES · JOSEPH SCHMITZ
CALIFORNIA STATE DEPARTMENT OF HEALTH

ISBN 0-917002-02-4

JOYCE MOTION PICTURE CO.
P.O. BOX 458 · NORTHRIDGE, CALIFORNIA 91324
PHONE (213) 885-7181

TABLE OF CONTENTS

the American
sign language alphabet

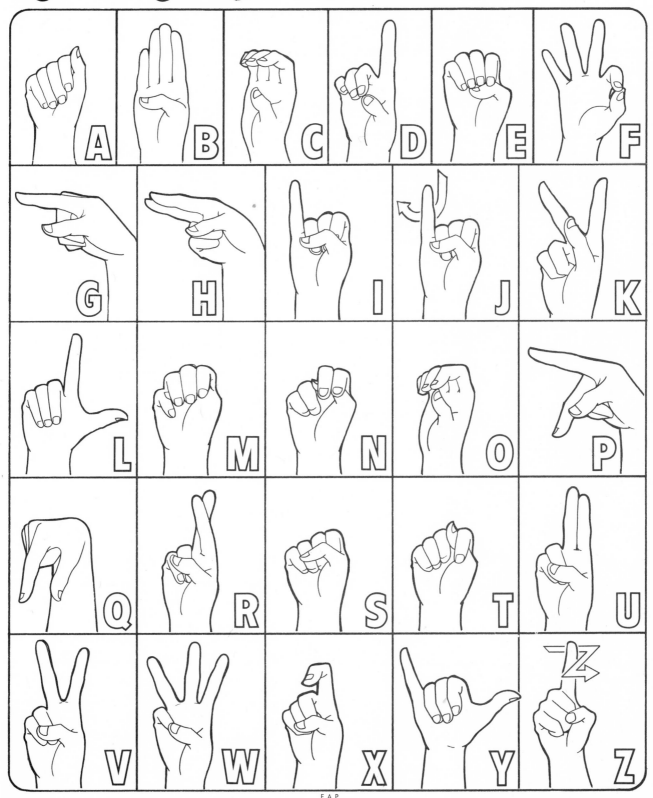

SELF, FAMILY, AND FRIENDS

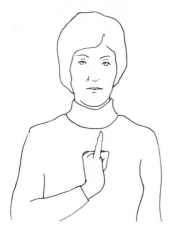

1
refers to self
I

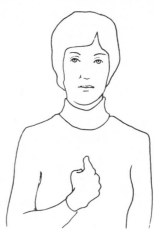

2
point to yourself
me

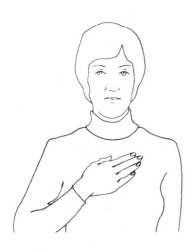

3
showing personal possession
my/mine

4
point to person
you

5
point to person
he/him -- she/her

6
person's possession
your / his / her

me   I

              you   my/mine

      your / his / her / hers   he/him -- she/her

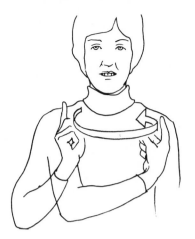

7
includes "you" and "me"

we

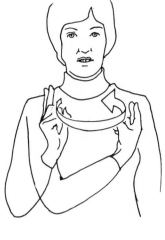

8
includes "you" and "me"

us

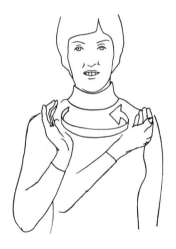

9.
includes persons in a group

our

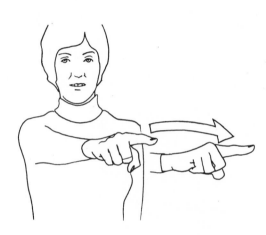

10
point to individual members in a group

they

11
refers to a baseball cap
note: all male signs made in this area

boy

12
refers to girl's bonnet string
note: all female signs made in this area

girl

us

we

they

our

girl

boy

13
female head of the family

mother

14
male head of the family

father

15
sign "girl" and "same"

sister

16
sign "boy" and "same"

brother

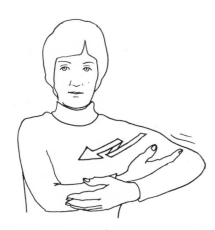

17
baby in your arms

baby

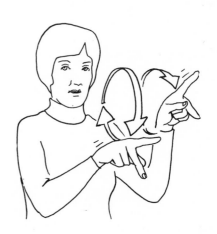

18
many persons

people

father

mother

brother

sister

people

baby

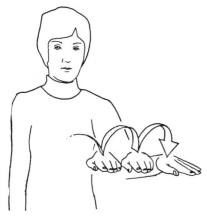

19
patting the heads of children
children

20
group sign using initial letter "F"
family

21
taking pulse
doctor

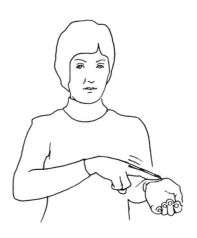

22
taking pulse
nurse

23
fixing teeth
dentist

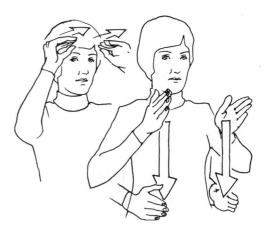

24
giving knowledge to others
teacher

family

children

nurse

doctor

teacher

dentist

25
taking pulse
technician

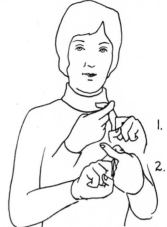

26
interlocking fingers indicate a
close relationship
friend

27
beard is outlined
Santa Claus

28
badge on the chest
policeman

29
"A" for am
am

30
"I" for is
is

friend

technician

policeman

Santa Claus

is

am

31
"R" for are
are

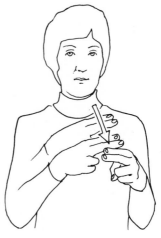

32
putting a name on a person or object
name

32A
motion originally from verb "to be",
now "B" for be
be

name   are

be

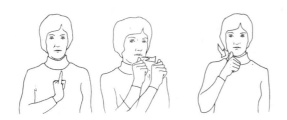

1. I   am   a   girl.

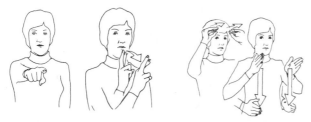

2. You   are   a   teacher.

3. My   sister   is   a   nurse.

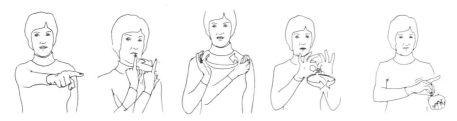

4. He   is   our   family   doctor.

5. My   brother   is   a   dentist.

16

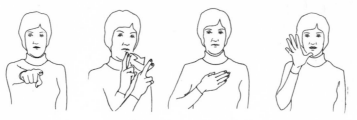

6. You   are   my   mother.

7. My   father   is   a   policeman.

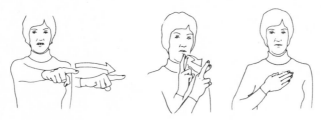

8. They   are   mine.

9. Santa Claus   is   our   friend.

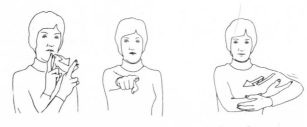

10. Are   you   a   baby?

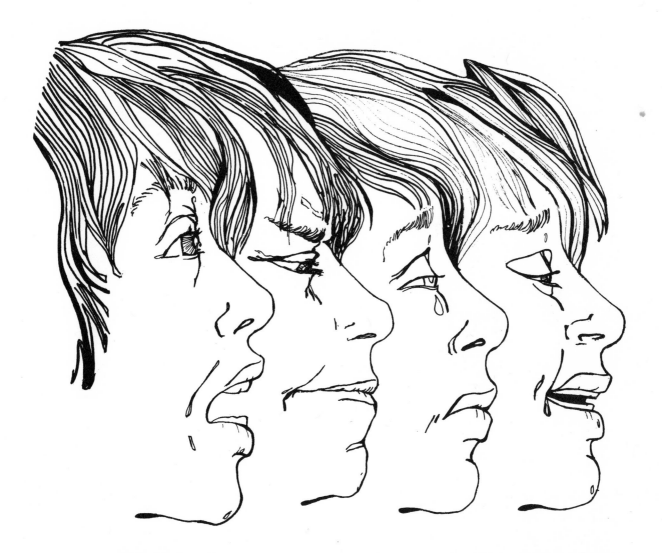

EMOTIONS AND FEELINGS

2

33
original idea - food was tasted, smelled
and offered as acceptable

good

34
original idea - food was tasted, smelled
and turned down

bad

35
feeling from the heart

happy

36
having a long face

sad

37
heart is being drawn out toward obje

like

38
close to one's heart

love

bad   good

sad   happy

love   like

39
indicates rejection
hate

40
refers to a dry throat
thirsty

41
an empty stomach
hungry

42
full stomach
full (feeling)

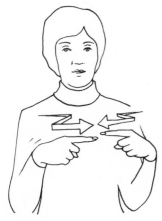

43
throbbing sensation
hurt/pain

44
showing areas of discomfort
sick/ill

thirsty

hate

full (feeling)

hungry

sick/ill

hurt/pain

45
blowing your nose

cold (illness)

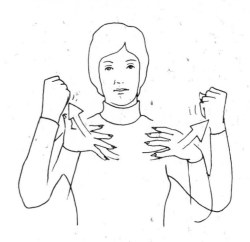

46
strong body

healthy/well

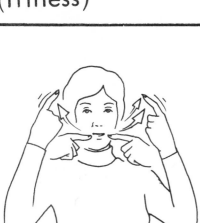

47
refers to mouth movements when laughing

laugh

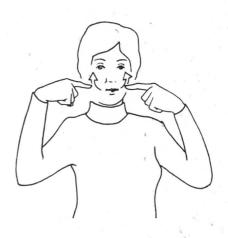

48
outline a smile

smile

49
tears running down face

cry

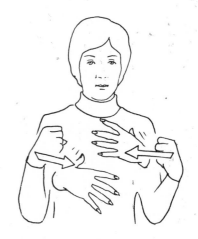

50
draw back in fear

afraid

healthy/well

cold (illness)

smile

laugh

afraid

cry

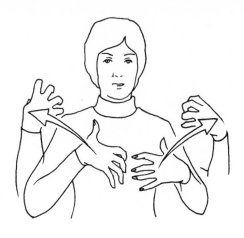

51
body filled with anger
angry

52
facial expression shows anger
mad

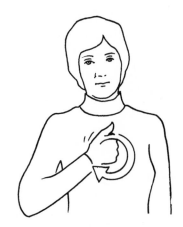

53
feeling remorse
sorry

54
rubbing chest in satisfaction
please

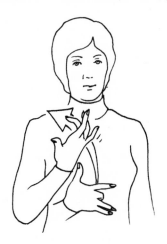

55
emotions from the heart
feel

94161

mad

angry

please

sorry

feel

1. I   am   afraid.

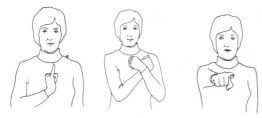

2. I   love   you.

3. I   feel   sick.

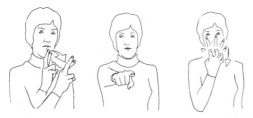

4. Are   you   mad?

5. He   is   a   bad   boy.

6. We   are   happy.

7. She   hurt   my   sister.

8. They   are   good children.

9. My   brother   likes   you.

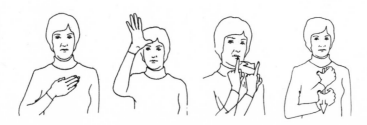

10. My   father   is   hungry.

WHAT WE DO
3

56
two doors opening

open

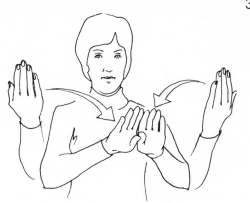

57
two doors closing

close

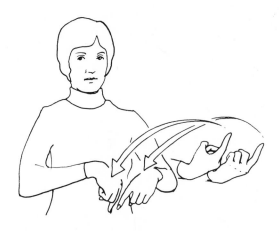

58
beckoning a person

come

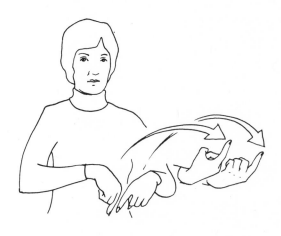

59
moving from one place to another

go

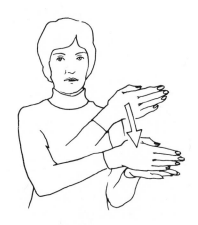

60
lowering railroad crossing gate

stop

61
remain here

stay

close   open

go   come

stay   stop

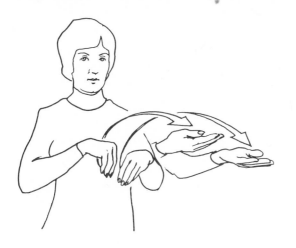

62
handing something to someone

give

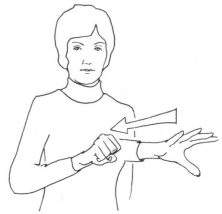

63
grasping something and bringing .
toward self

take

64
fingers represent legs standing
on floor

stand

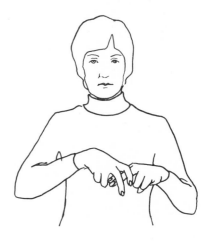

65
fingers represent legs hanging over
edge of chair

sit

66
hands represent feet walking

walk

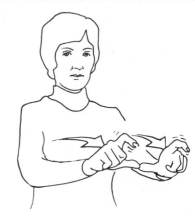

67
fingers represent two legs in a
running motion

run

take   give

sit   stand

run   walk

68
fingers represent legs jumping

jump

69
fingers represent person falling

fall

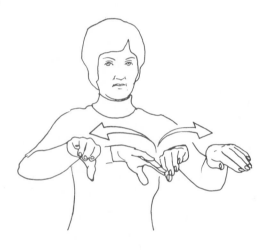

70
motion of swimming

swim

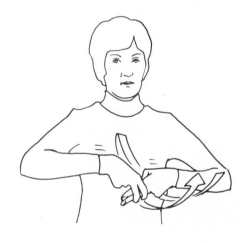

71
moving back and forth

swing

72
climbing a ladder

climb

73
fingers represent feet dancing
across floor

dance

fall

jump

swing

swim

dance

climb

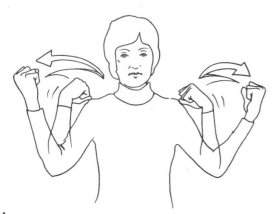

74
arm exercise
exercise

75
dropping an imaginary object
drop

76
picking up something with hand
pick up

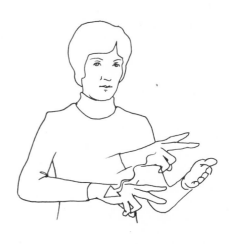

77
following the lines of an imaginary
page from left to right
read

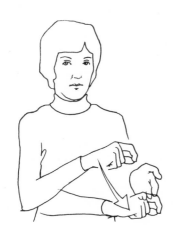

78
writing with an imaginary pencil
write

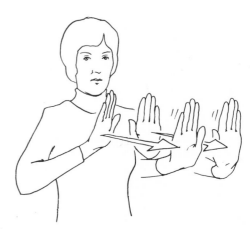

79
push an imaginary object
push

drop

exercise

read

pick up

push

write

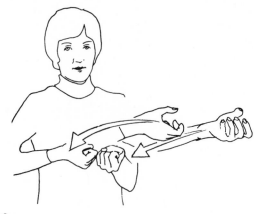

80
pulling something toward self
pull

81
slaves being cuffed together
work

82
motion indicates activity
play

83
two fingertips represent eyes looking
from place to place
look/watch

84
eyes looking forward
see

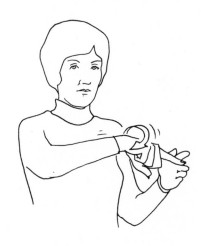

85
key being turned
start/begin

work

pull

look/watch

play

start/begin

see

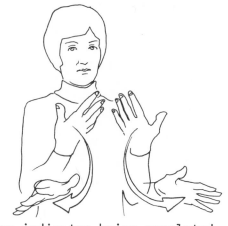

86
motion indicates being completed
or ended
finish

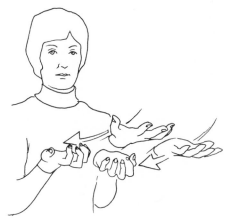

87
drawing toward self indicates desire
want

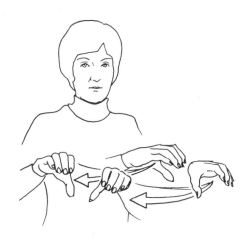

88
action of doing something
do

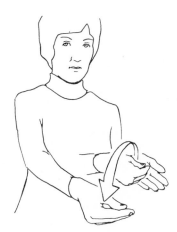

89
giving out money for something
buy

90
peeling out money from a roll of bills
pay

91
taking knowledge from a book and putting
it in your head
learn

want

finish

buy

do

learn

pay

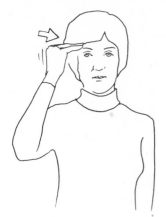

92
have knowledge in the head

know

93
the "light bulb" in head turning on

understand

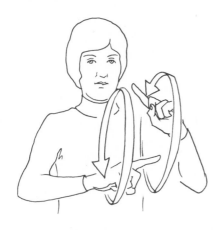

94
indicates motion of hands while signing

sign

95
two people talking back and forth

talk

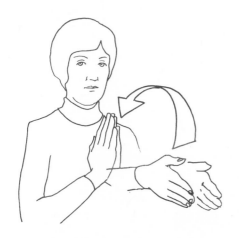

96
hands held as in prayer

ask

97
words from the mouth

tell

understand   know

talk   sign

tell   ask

98
breaking something in half
break

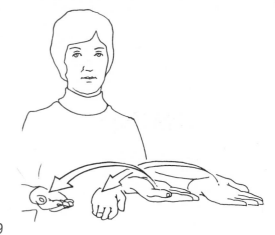

99
bringing an object toward self
bring

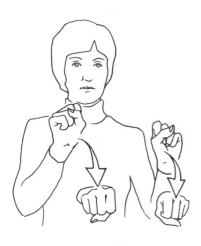

100
nodding of hands with determination
can

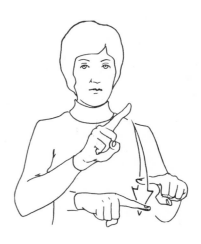

101
push down, away
can't

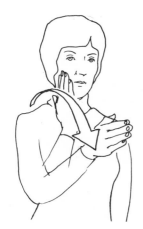

102
indicates future time
will

103
changing positions
change

bring   break

can't   can

change   will

104
scissors cutting paper

cut/scissors

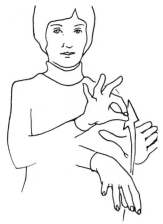

105
picking up an object

find

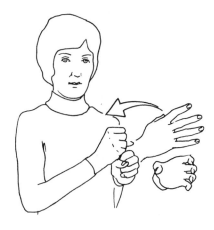

106
grasp and hold object

get

107
holding object close to one's self

have

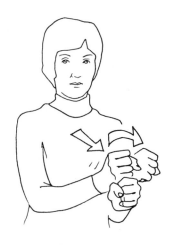

108
forming something with hands

make

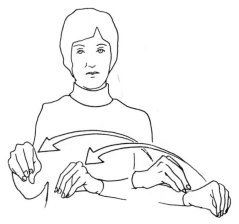

109
move object from one place to another

move

find

cut/scissors

have

get

move

make

110
motion of throwing

throw

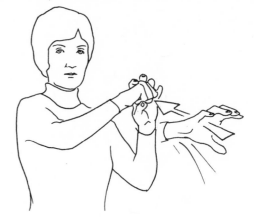

111
catching a ball

catch

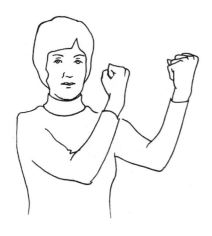

112
motion of fighting

fight

113
shortened from original sign of man
helping a woman across the street

help

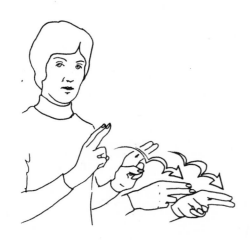

114
motion of being fast

hurry

115
placing a kiss on the cheek

kiss

catch

throw

help

fight

kiss

hurry

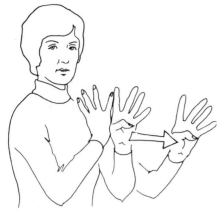

116
people standing in a line
line up

117
pouring from a pitcher into a glass
pour

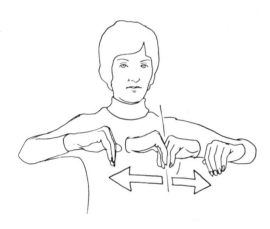

118
pulling something apart
separate

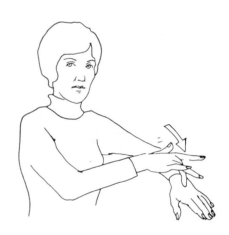

119
touching something
touch

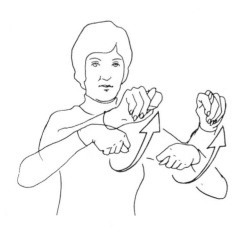

120
forward motion indicates effort
try

121
continuing motion to represent
frequent use
use

pour

line up

touch

separate

use

try

122
motion in place until ready to
move forward

wait

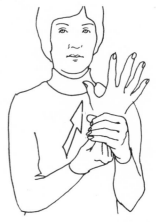

123
something coming out of the ground

grow

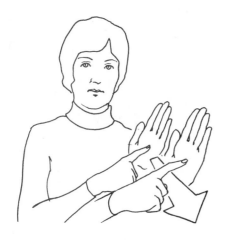

124
pointing out something

show

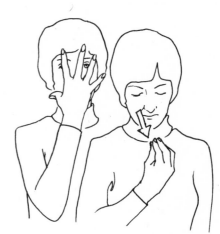

125
eyes closed

sleep

126
eyes open

wake up

grow

wait

sleep

show

wake up

1. I am finished.

2. My friend kissed your mother.

3. He is angry.

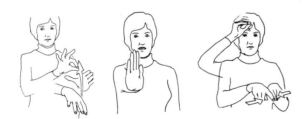

4. Find your brother.

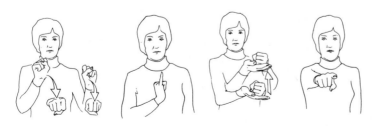

5. Can I help you?

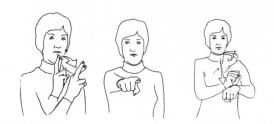

6. Are   you working ?

7. My   sister   pushed   me.

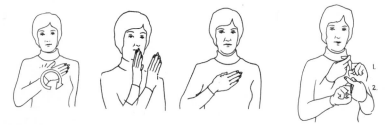

8. Please   be   my   friend.

9. They   are   swimming.

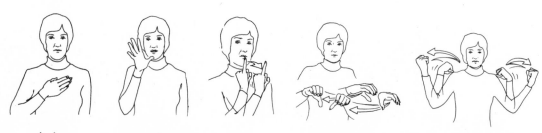

10. My   mother   is   doing   exercises.

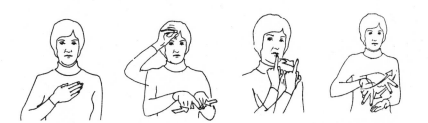

11. My   brother   is   dancing.

12. She   has   a   cold.

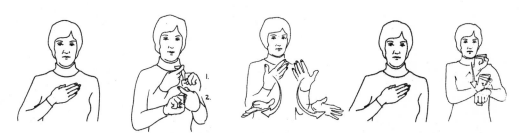

13. My   friend   finished   my   work.

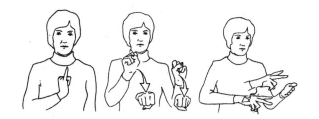

14. I   can   read.

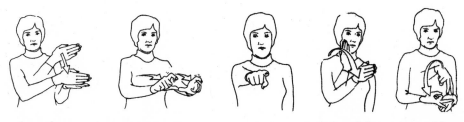

15. Stop   running;   you   will   fall.

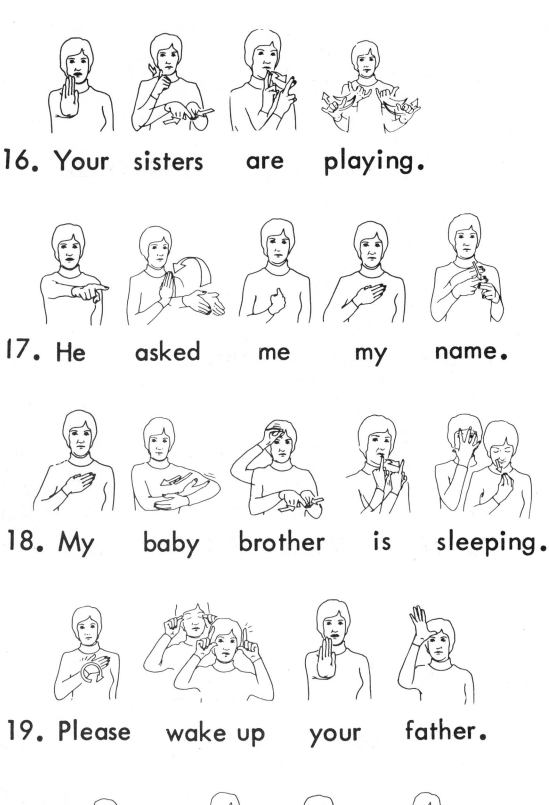

16. Your sisters are playing.

17. He asked me my name.

18. My baby brother is sleeping.

19. Please wake up your father.

20. Exercise makes you healthy.

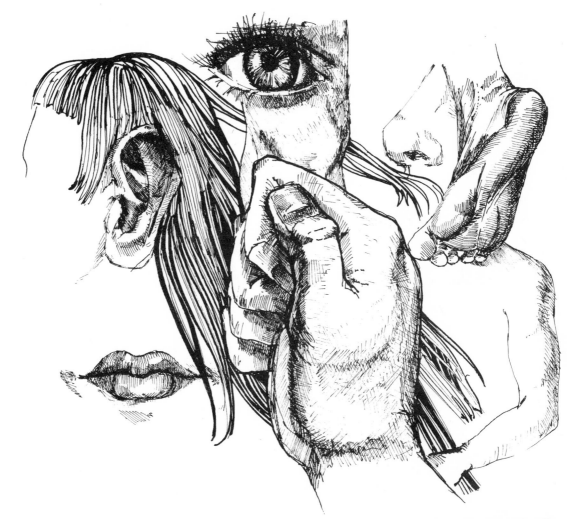

BODY PARTS
4

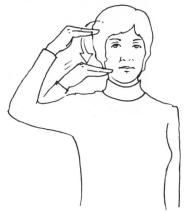

127
frame the face from temple to chin
head

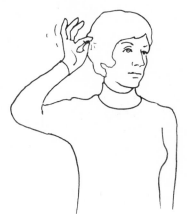

128
touch hair
hair

129
outline face
face

130
point to eye
eye

131
point to nose
nose

132
point to mouth
mouth

hair

head

eye

face

mouth

nose

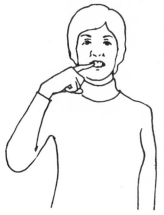

133
point to teeth
teeth

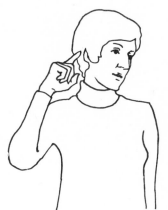

134
point to ear
ear

135
point to neck
neck

136
point to arm
arm

137
point to hand
hand

138
point to finger
finger

ear   teeth

arm   neck

finger   hand

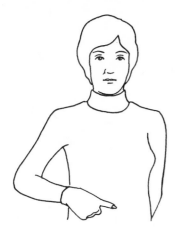

139
point to stomach
stomach

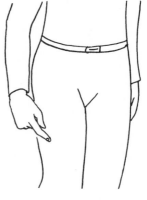

140
point to leg
leg

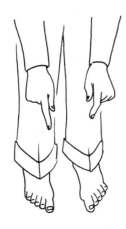

141
point to feet
feet

141-A
motion of eyes closing
close eyes

leg

stomach

close eyes

feet

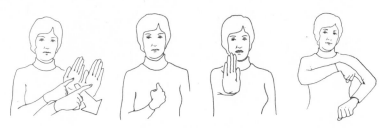

1. Show   me   your   arm.

2. My   stomach hurts.

3. Close your eyes.

4. Find   your   ears.

5. My   sister   hurt   her   finger.

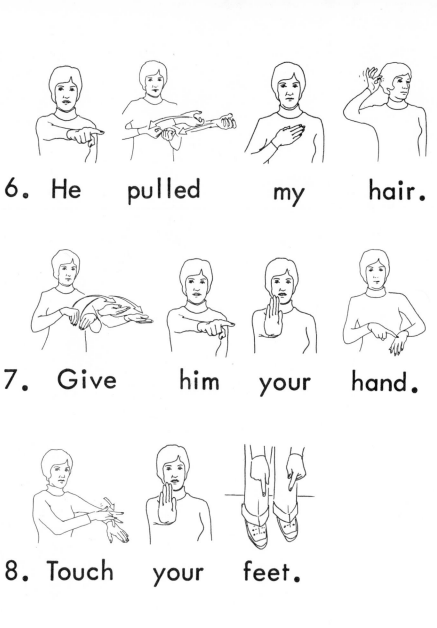

6. He   pulled   my   hair.

7. Give   him   your   hand.

8. Touch   your   feet.

9. Show   me   your   teeth.

10. Touch   your   nose.

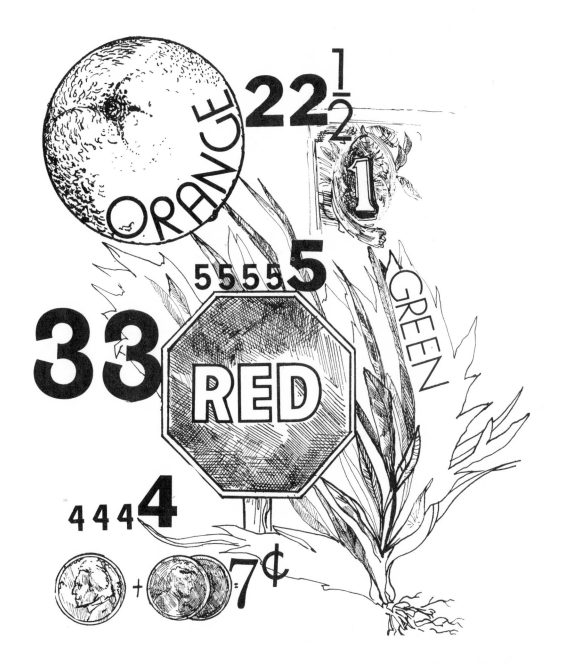

22$\frac{1}{2}$

ORANGE

1

GREEN

5555 **5**

33

RED

444**4**

+ 7¢

COLORS AND NUMBERS

5

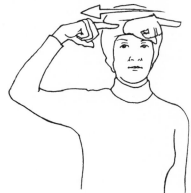

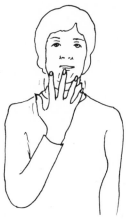

142
Represents color spectrum of rainbow.
color

143
Indicates dark eyebrows.
black

144
Indicates dark skin.
brown

145
Lipstick on the lips.
red

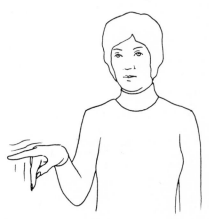

146
Pink lips.
pink

147
emphasis on the first letter of
the word
purple

black

color

red

brown

purple

pink

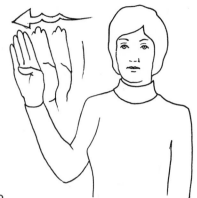

148
emphasis on the first letter of the word

blue

149
emphasis on the first letter of the word

green

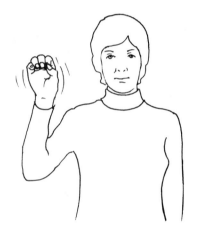

150
emphasis on the first letter of the word

orange

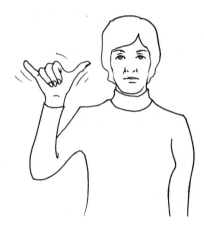

151
emphasis on the first letter of the word

yellow

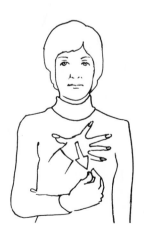

152
shows color of a white T-shirt

white

153
"0"

zero

green

blue

yellow

orange

zero

white

154
one finger

one

155
two fingers

two

156
two fingers and thumb

three

157
four fingers

four

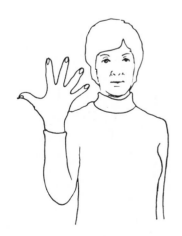

158
five fingers

five

159
thumb and fourth finger

six

two

one

four

three

six

five

160
thumb and third finger

seven

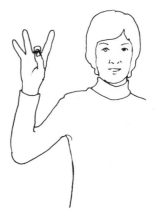

161
thumb and middle finger

eight

162
thumb and index finger

nine

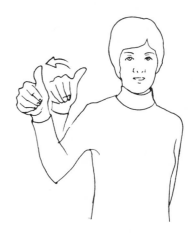

163
fist, thumb up

ten

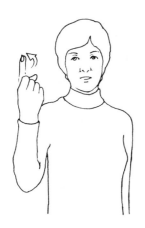

164
fist, index finger

eleven

165
fist, index and middle fingers

twelve

eight

seven

ten

nine

twelve

eleven

1. Our teacher has blue eyes.

2. Your sister has five children.

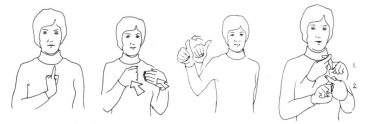

3. I have ten friends.

4. I saw twelve boys playing.

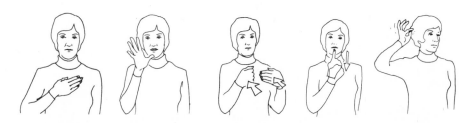

5. My mother has red hair.

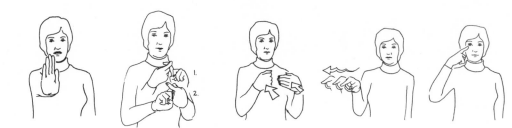

6. Your friend has green eyes.

7. My brother has brown hair.

8. She has seven brothers.

9. Father has brown eyes.

10. Your father has three children.

CLOTHING
6

83

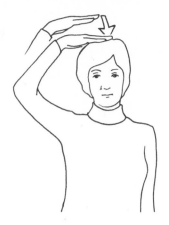

166
covering on the head
hat

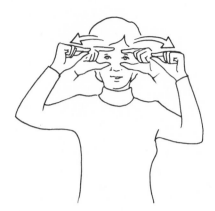

167
outline glasses on face
glasses

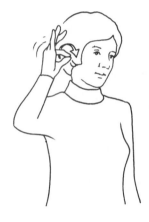

168
inserting earmold into ear
hearing aid

169
outline
collar

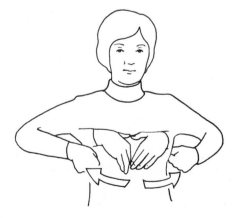

170
outline bra on person
bra

171
hand grasps shirt
shirt

glasses

hat

collar

hearing aid

shirt

bra

172
outline lapels of coat

coat/sweater

173
buckling your belt

belt

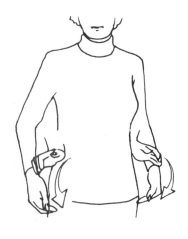

174
old fashioned bloomers

panties

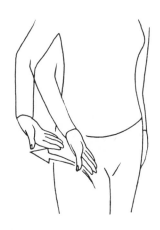

175
outline legs of shorts

undershorts

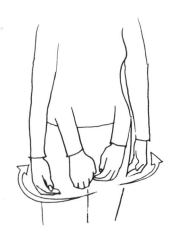

176
short pants

shorts

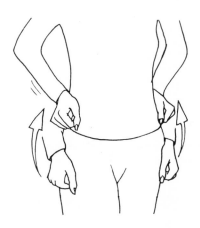

177
pulling up pair of pants

pants

belt   coat/sweater

undershorts   panties

pants   shorts

178
the knitting of socks

socks

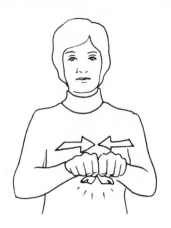

179
heels of shoes clicking together

shoes

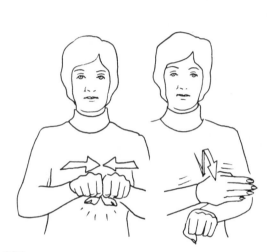

180
high shoes

boots

181
feeling the material

clothes/dress

88

shoes

socks

clothes/dress

boots

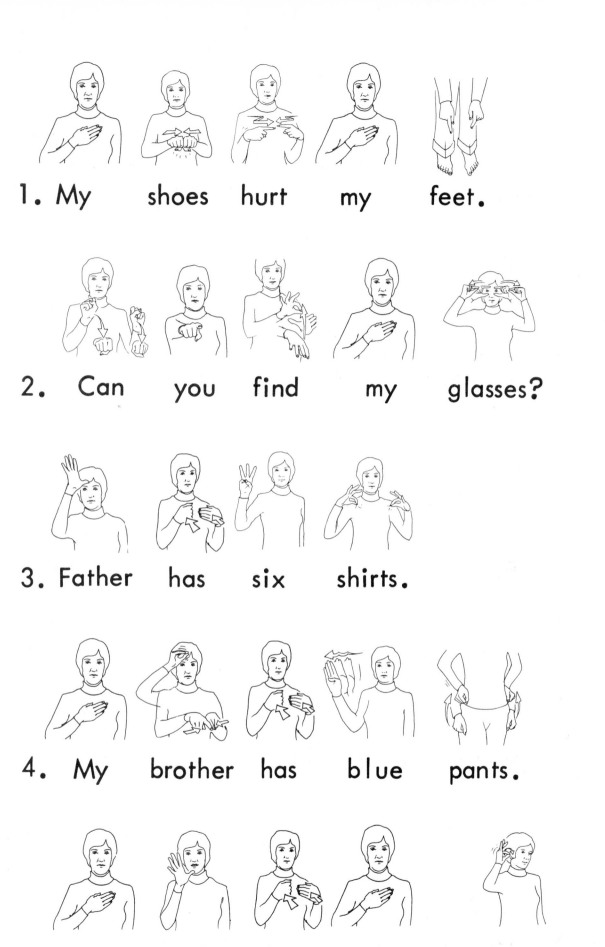

1. My shoes hurt my feet.

2. Can you find my glasses?

3. Father has six shirts.

4. My brother has blue pants.

5. My mother has my hearing aid.

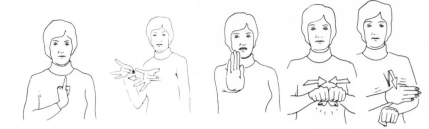

6. I   like   your   boots.

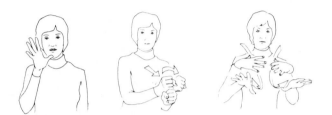

7. Mother   made   a   dress.

8. My   sister   has   a   blue   coat.

9. Santa Claus   has   a   red   hat.

10. I   have   a   white   belt.

GROOMING
7

182
washing the body

bathe

183
water coming from the shower head

shower

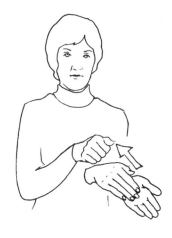

184
rubbing soap to get lather

soap

185
washing face with the palms of
hands

wash face

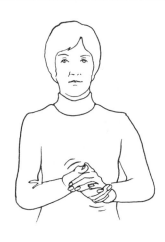

186
rub hands together

wash hands

187
wiping moisture from body

dry

shower

bathe

wash face

soap

dry

wash hands

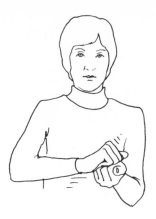

188
washing something
wash

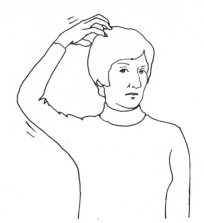

189
fingers represent teeth of comb
comb hair

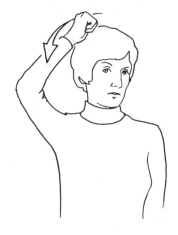

190
closed hand represents hair brush
brush hair

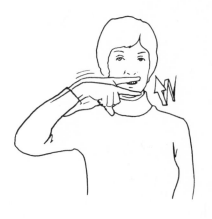

191
index finger represents tooth brush
brush teeth

192
shaving with a razor
shave

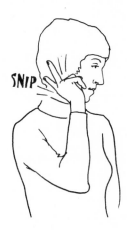

193
motion of cutting hair
haircut

comb hair

wash

brush teeth

brush hair

haircut

shave

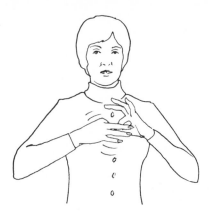

194
motion of buttoning

button

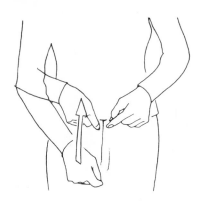

195
motion of zipping garment

zip

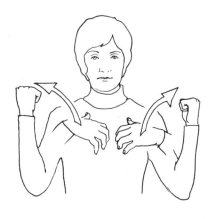

196
removing garment

take off

197
hanging garment on a hook

hang up

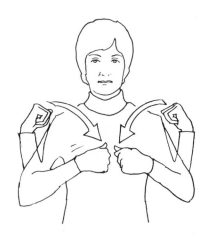

198
putting on garment

put on

zip

button

hang up

take off

put on

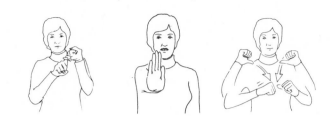

1. Hang up   your   coat.

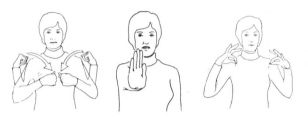

2. Put on   your   shirt.

3. Brush your teeth.

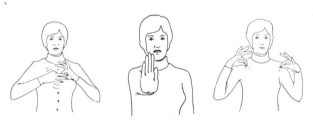

4. Button   your   shirt.

5. Comb your hair.

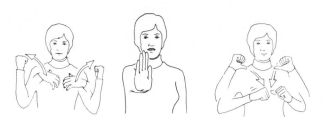

6. Take off   your   sweater.

7. I   will   take a shower.

8. Wash your face.

9. Zip your pants.

10. Please   wash   my   socks.

AT THE TABLE

8

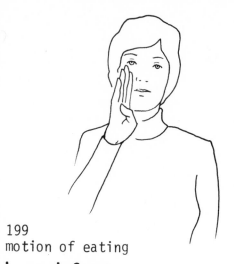

199
motion of eating
breakfast

200
motion of eating
lunch

201
motion of eating
dinner

202
cutting motion
knife / cut

203
tines of a fork
fork

204
motion of eating with a spoon
spoon

lunch

breakfast

knife / cut

dinner

spoon

fork

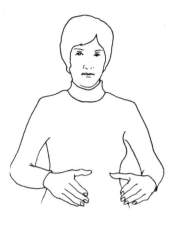

205
outline shape of a plate

plate

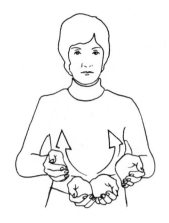

206
outline of a bowl

bowl

207
outline of a cup

cup

208
indicates height of glass

glass

209
wiping corners of mouth

napkin

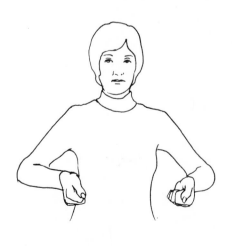

210
holding an imaginary tray

tray

bowl

plate

glass

cup

tray

napkin

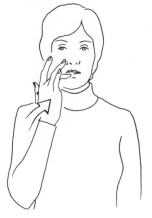

211
putting food in mouth

taste

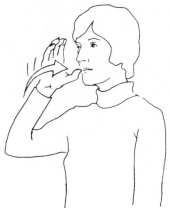

212
drinking from a glass

drink

213
smelling something

smell

214
tasting something on end of finger

eat/food

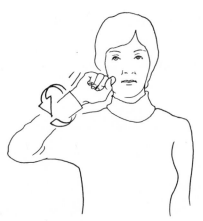

215
coring an apple

apple

216
squeezing juice from an orange into mouth

orange

drink

taste

eat/food

smell

orange

apple

217
peeling a banana
banana

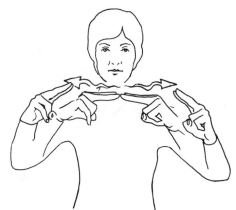

218
shows outline of a strip of cooked bacon
bacon

219
cracking an egg open
egg

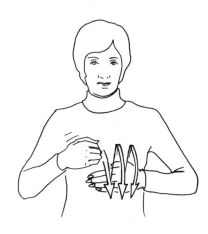

220
slicing a loaf of bread
bread

221
old fashioned way of toasting bread on a fork
toast

222
buttering bread
butter

bacon

banana

bread

egg

butter

toast

223
forming a hamburger patty
hamburger

224
links of weiners
hot dog

225
two pieces of bread together
sandwich

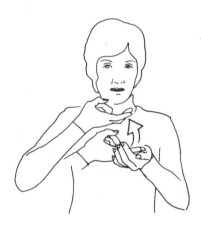

226
taking soup with a spoon
soup

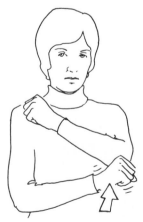

227
old European custom of hitting crackers
with elbow allowing crumbs to fall into
soup
crackers

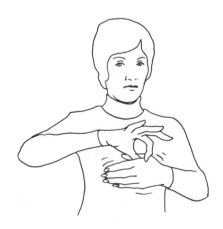

228
side of beef hanging on a meat hook
meat

112

hot dog

hamburger

soup

sandwich

meat

crackers

229
piercing a potato with a fork

potato

230
eating corn on the cob

corn

231
"W" indicates water for drinking

water

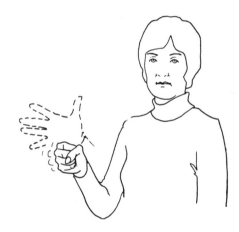

232
milking a cow

milk

233
grinding coffee beans

coffee

234
stirring a teabag in a cup

tea

113

corn

potato

milk

water

tea

coffee

235
a shot in the arm for energy
coke/pop

236
cutting a piece of cake
cake

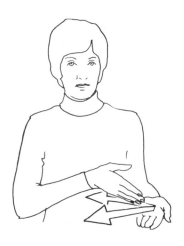

237
cutting a piece of pie
pie

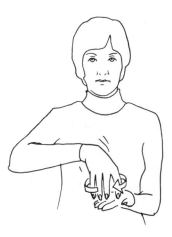

238
using a cookie cutter
cookie

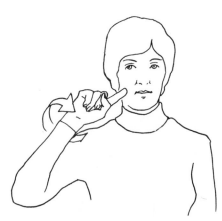

239
having a sweet tooth
candy

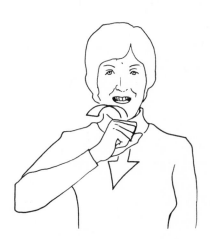

240
licking an ice cream cone
ice cream

cake   coke/pop

cookie   pie

ice cream   candy

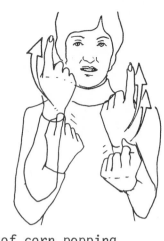

241
motion of corn popping

popcorn

242
motion of teeth while chewing gum

gum

243
sweet tasting

sugar

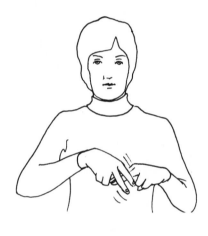

244
old fashioned method of sprinkling
salt on food

salt

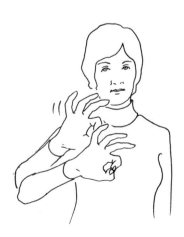

245
shaking pepper on food

pepper

gum

popcorn

salt

sugar

pepper

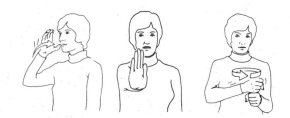

1. Drink your coffee.

2. Butter your bread.

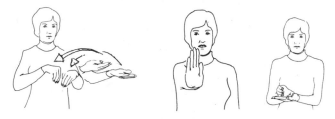

3. Give me your cup.

4. I like hamburgers.

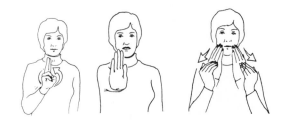

5. your napkin.

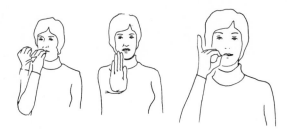

6. Eat your dinner.

7. Your pie is good.

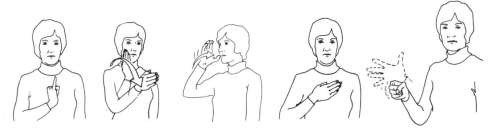

8. I will drink my milk.

9. Your food smells good.

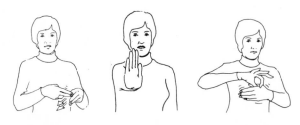

10. Cut your meat.

AROUND THE HOUSE
9

246
head on pillow
bed

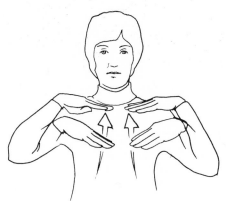

247
pulling blanket over self
blanket

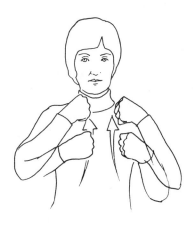

248
pulling sheet over self
sheet

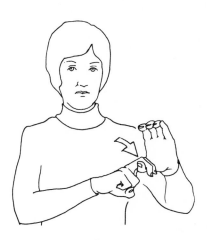

249
"C" is chair, other hand represents
legs in sitting position
chair

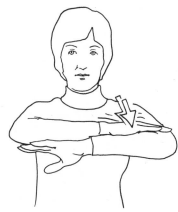

250
resting arms on an imaginary table
table/desk

251
opening and closing a window
window

blanket

bed

chair

sheet

window

table/desk

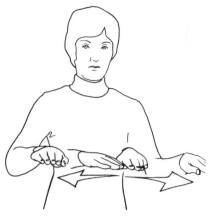

252
a flat surface
floor

253
opening a door
door

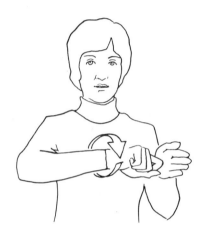

254
turning key in a lock
key

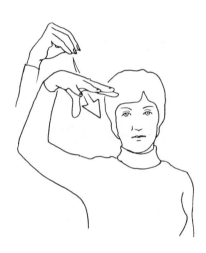

255
light shining down
lamp/light

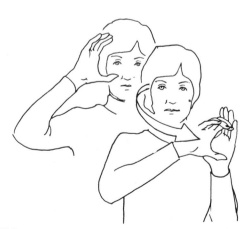

256
taking picture and transferring it on paper
picture

257
first letter represents the word
bathroom/toilet

door

floor

lamp/light

key

bathroom/toilet

picture

127

258
abbreviated to "TV"

television

259
holding phone to the ear

telephone

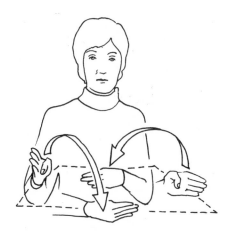

260
sides of box

box

261
sweeping floor

broom/sweep

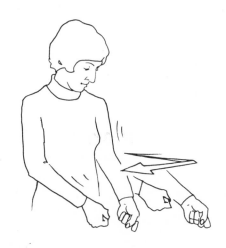

262
washing floor

mop

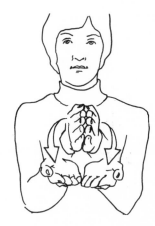

263
hands are front and back covers of
book being opened

book

telephone

television

broom/sweep

box

book

mop

264
many sentences strung together
story

265
movement of paper through a machine
paper

266
motion of writing
pencil

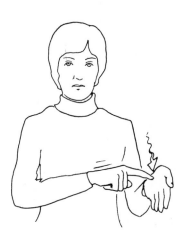

267
motion of drawing
crayon

268
putting stamp on an envelope
letter

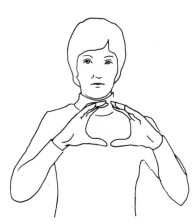

269
outline of ball
ball

paper

story

crayon

pencil

ball

letter

270
motion is like "play" but with initial
"T"

toy

271
a flag waving in the air

flag

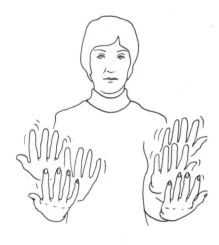

272
flames rising

fire

273
water from the sky

rain

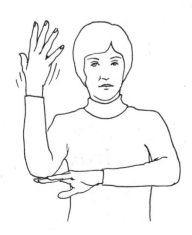

274
arm represents tree trunk, fingers
branches

tree

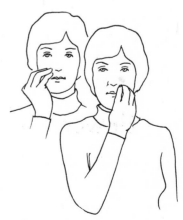

275
smelling flower

flower

flag

toy

rain

fire

flower

tree

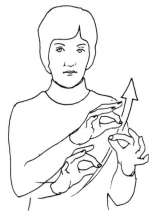

276
motion of sewing
sew

277
Holding coins and bills in hand.
money

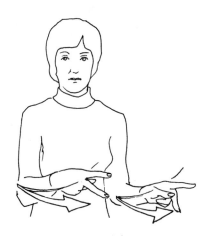

278
Motion is like "play" but with letter "P".
party

279
druggist grinding with mortar and pestle
medicine

money

sew

medicine

party

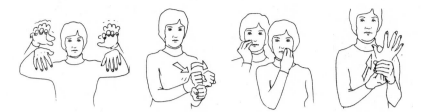

1. Rain   makes   flowers   grow.

2. We   are   having a   party.

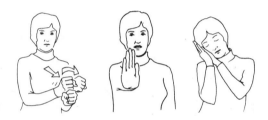

3. Make   your   bed.

4. Your   door   is   open.

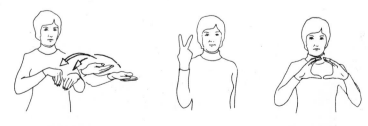

5. Give me   two   balls.

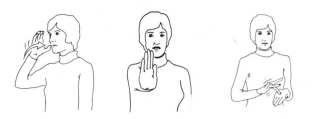

6. Drink   your   medicine.

7. Please   give me   your   key.

8. Bring   me   your   red   ball.

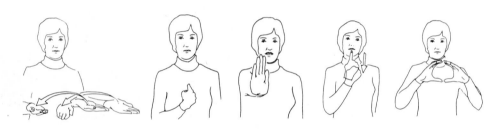

9. You   have   a   purple   box.

10. I   have a pink blanket.

WHERE WE ARE

10

280
place where you eat and sleep

home

281
outline roof and sides of house

house

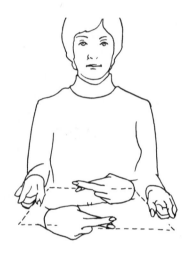

282
outline four sides of room
with the "R" hand.

room

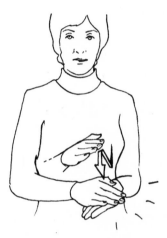

283
teacher clapping for attention

school

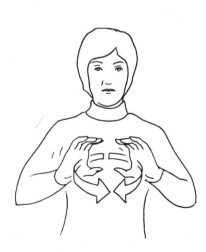

284
students in a group

class

285
flat hand represents rock and "C"
the church

church

house

home

school

room

church

class

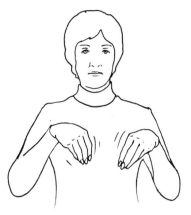

286
pushing wares on potential customers
store

287
symbol of the International Red Cross
hospital

288
many houses in a row
town

289
showing beard of farmer
farm

290
outline of area with initial "P"
place

291
old time movie flicks
movie

hospital

store

farm

town

movie

place

292
putting something into the hand

in

293
taking something out of the hand

out

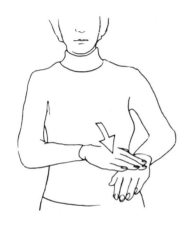

294
one thing on top of another

on

295
removing something from the top of
another

off

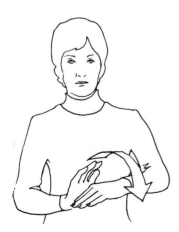

296
to go across something

over

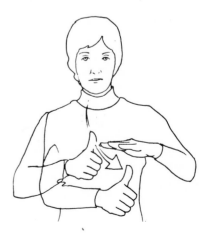

297
to go below something

under

out

in

off

on

under

over

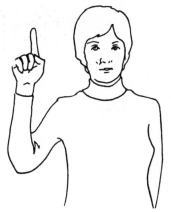

298
showing direction <u>up</u>

299
showing direction <u>down</u>
down

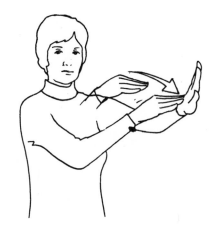

300
going toward something
at

301
to go around something
around

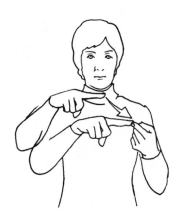

302
moving toward something
to

303
immediate area
here

down   up

around   at

here   to

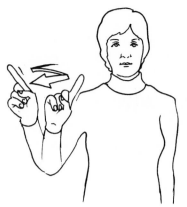

304
point from one area to another

where

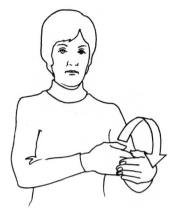

305
from one thing to another

next

next   where

1. Father works in a hospital.

2. Where are my brown shoes?

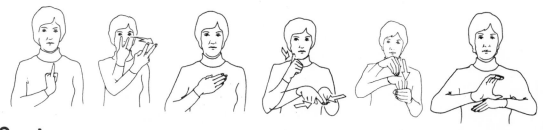

3. I saw my sister in church.

4. My mother is home.

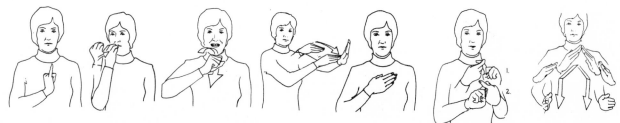

5. I ate ice cream at my friend's house.

6. We saw a good movie.

7. I saw a policeman at school.

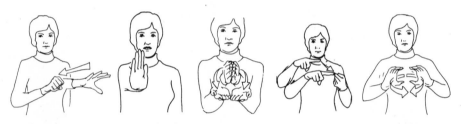

8. Take your book to class.

9. Her house is yellow.

10. Father is in town.

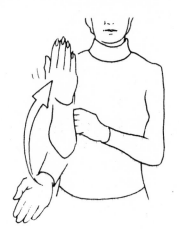

306
watch on wrist
time

307
sun coming up
morning

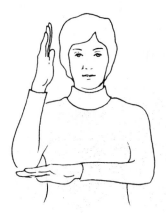

308
sun at midday
noon

309
sun on its way down
afternoon

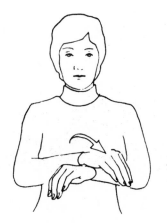

310
sun gone down over the horizon
night

311
outline of a quarter moon
moon

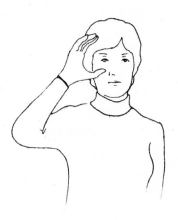

morning

time

afternoon

noon

moon

night

312
sun rising and setting
day

313
outline shape of sun
sun

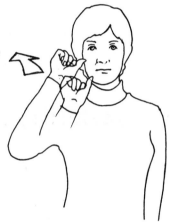

314
backward motion to indicate past
tense
yesterday

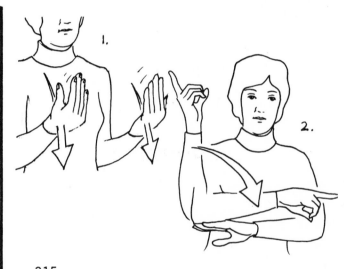

315
sign "now" and "day"
today

316
forward motion to indicate future
tomorrow

317
at the immediate time
now

sun

day

today

yesterday

now

tomorrow

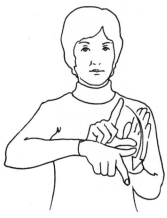

318
when hands of clock have moved ahead

later

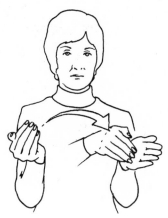

319
repeat it once more

again

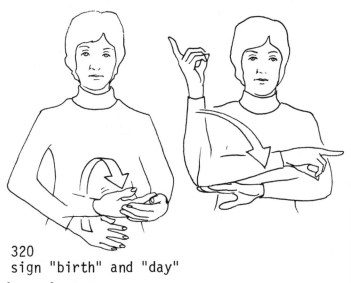

320
sign "birth" and "day"

birthday

321
shows top arch of a Christmas wreath

Christmas

again

later

Christmas

birthday

1.　　Today　　　　is　　your　　　birthday.

2.　I　　will　　see　　you　　tomorrow　　night.

3.　We　　eat　　our　　lunch　　at　　　noon.

4.　Good morning.

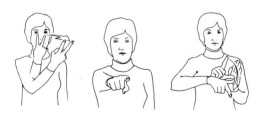

5.　See　　you　　later.

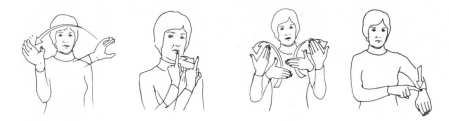

6. Christmas   is a happy   time.

7. Can   you   come   home   today ?

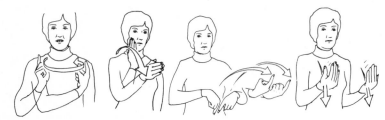

8. We   will   go   now.

9. Good night.

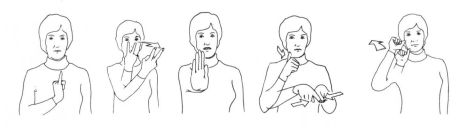

10. I   saw   your   sister yesterday.

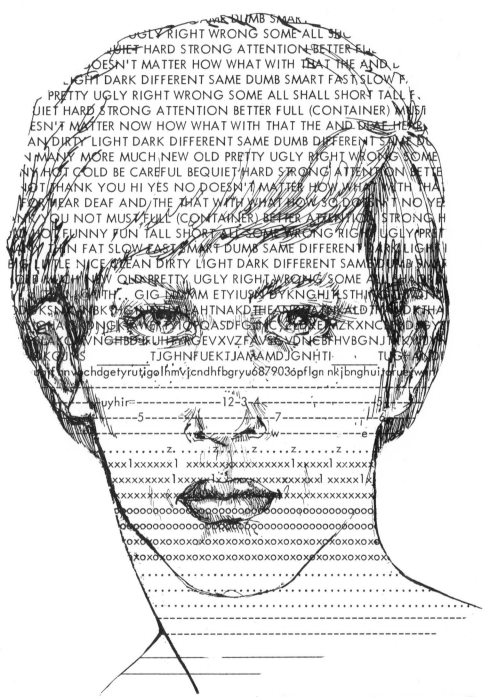

DAILY LIVING

12

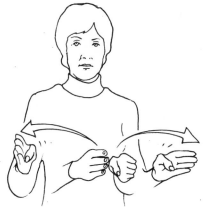

322
showing size of object
big

323
showing size of object
little

324
wiping something clean
clean

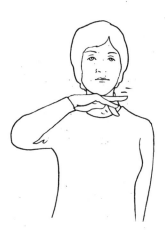

325
food dripping from chin
dirty

326
rays of light
light/clear

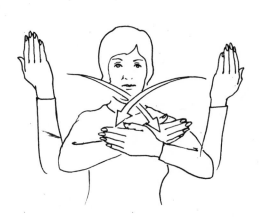

327
darkness closing in around you
dark

little   big

dirty   clean

dark   light/clear

328
two objects that are not alike

different

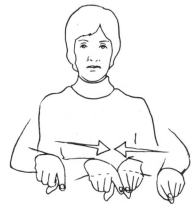

329
two identical objects

same

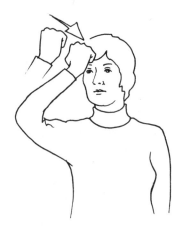

330
hard to penetrate

dumb

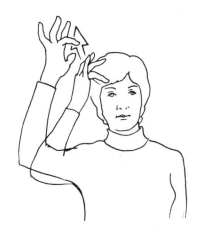

331
good ideas from the head

smart

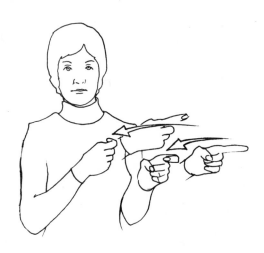

332
gun recoiling when bullet leaves

fast

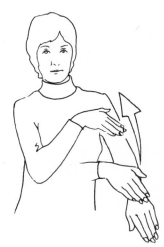

333
something moving slowly

slow

same   different

smart   dumb

slow   fast

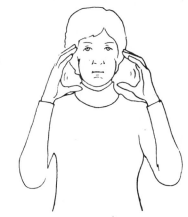

334
puffy cheeks
fat

335
hollow cheeks
thin

336
motion indicates a great many numbers
many

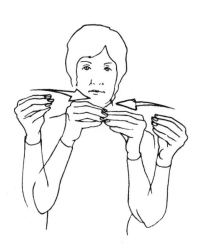

337
adding more to something
more

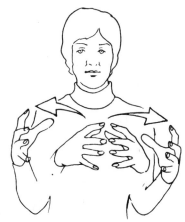

338
a large quantity of something
much

339
something smooth or untouched
new

thin

fat

more

many

new

much

169

340
beard indicates age

old

341
attractive face

pretty

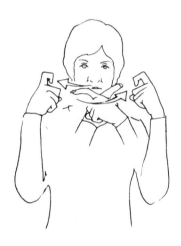

342
masking the face

ugly

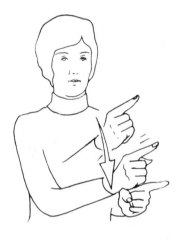

343
two things lined up exactly right

right

344
facial expression indicates error

wrong

345
removing part from the whole

some

pretty   old

right   ugly

some   wrong

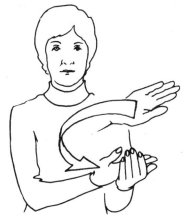

346
gathering everything or everyone together
all

347
the height of a person
short

348
the height of a person
tall

349
funny nose of clown being given to another
fun

350
funny nose of clown
funny

351
throw something hot out of mouth
hot

short

all

fun

tall

hot

funny

352
motion of shivering
cold (weather)

353
fingers represent eyes watching
for hazards
be careful

354
stop talking
be quiet

355
hitting something hard
hard

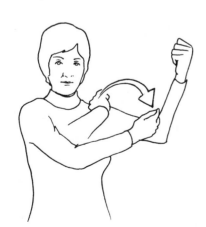

356
shows the size of arm muscles
strong

357
all attention is focused on one object
like blinders on a horse
attention

be careful   cold (weather)

hard   be quiet

attention   strong

358
hand moved upward represents higher quality
better

359
container filled to top
full (container)

360
motion indicates urgency
must

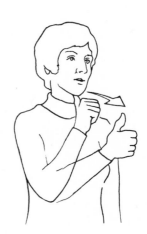

361
gesture of negation
not

362
blowing a kiss in appreciation
thank you

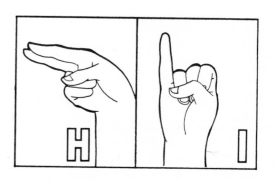

363
fingerspelled
hi

full (container)   better

not   must

hi   thank you

364
hand represents nodding head

yes

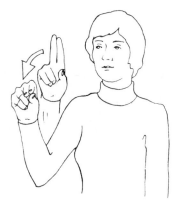

365
abbreviated <u>NO</u>

no

366
able to go either way

doesn't matter

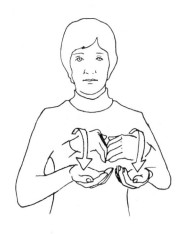

367
change of hand positions and <u>how</u>
it happened

how

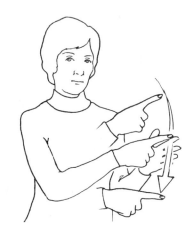

58
ngers represent several ideas from
ich to choose

/hat

369
putting two objects together

with

no   yes

how   doesn't matter

with   what

370
the object away from you
that

371
new sign built on the sign for
"that"
the

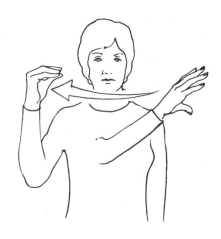

372
stretching out words
and

373
ears closed
deaf

374
indicates area of hearing
hear

375
thoughts from head
for

the   that

deaf   and

for   hear

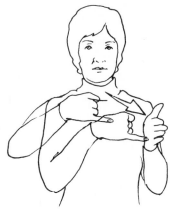

376
pointing to something in your hand

it

it

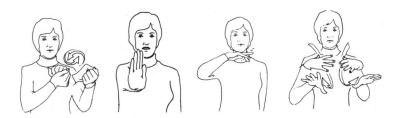

1. Change your dirty clothes.

2. Your glass is full.

3. She ate many cookies.

4. Your new dress is pretty.

5. You are a smart boy.

6. The   house   is   on fire.

7. The   yellow   flowers   are   pretty.

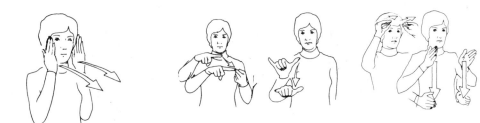

8. Pay attention   to   the   teacher.

The   girl   is   fat.

10. My   mother   has   a   clean   house.

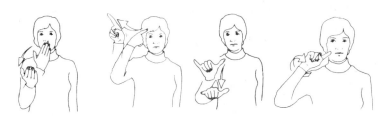

11. Thank you   for   the   candy.

12. I   feel   better   today.

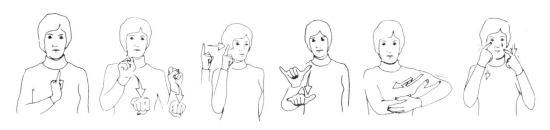

13. I   can   hear   the   baby   crying.

14. You   must   brush your hair.

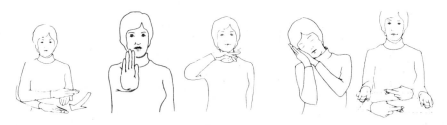

15. Clean   your   dirty   bedroom.

16. The   corn   is   growing   tall.

17. I   am   sick   again.

18. Time   to go   to   school.

19. That   is   not   your   book.

20. What   time   will   you   come   tomorrow ?

ANIMALS
13

377
bird's beak opening and closing
bird

378
eating grain
chicken

379
wide bill opening and closing
duck

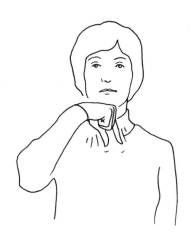

380
the wattle of the turkey
turkey

381
whiskers on cheeks
cat

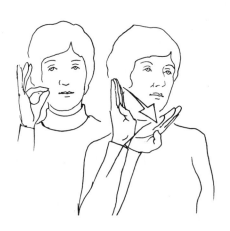

382
swatting bees away from cheek
bees

chicken

bird

turkey

duck

bees

cat

383
mouse's nose twitching
mouse

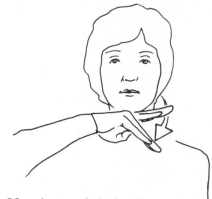

384
originally done with hand moving
forward to show motion of pig's
snout, now done sideways
pig

385
ears of horse
horse

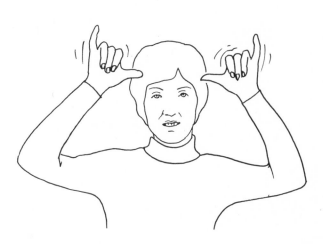

386
horns of cow
cow

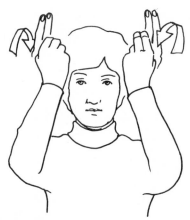

387
ears of rabbit
rabbit

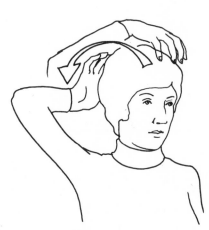

388
outline lion's mane
lion

pig   mouse

cow   horse

lion   rabbit

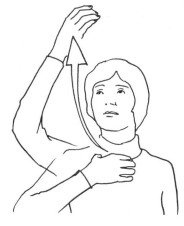

389
long neck of giraffe

giraffe

390
trunk of elephant

elephant

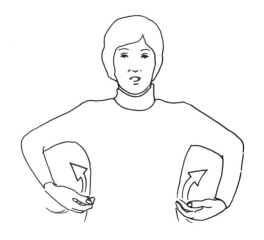

391
scratching for fleas

monkey

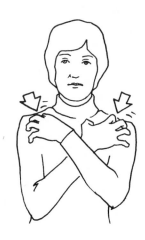

392
a bear scratching in crossed arm
position

bear

393
swimming through water

fish

394
shearing sheep's wool

sheep

elephant

giraffe

bear

monkey

sheep

fish

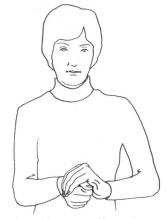

395
head moving from under its shell
turtle

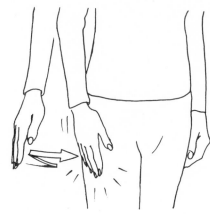

396
call a dog
dog

397
lungs of an animal breathing
animal

dog

turtle

animal

1. I   see   eight chickens.

2. Play   with   the   big   brown   dog.

3. Monkeys climb   trees.

4. Our   cat   is   sick.

5. The   baby   duck   is   yellow.

6. The   giraffe   is   tall.

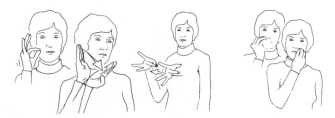

7. Bees   like   flowers.

8. Elephants   are   strong.

9. Lions   eat   meat.

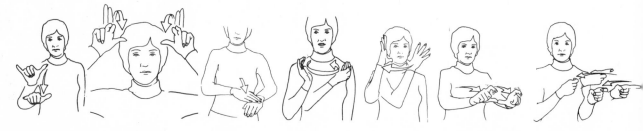

10. The horses   on   our   farm   run   fast.

TRANSPORTATION
14

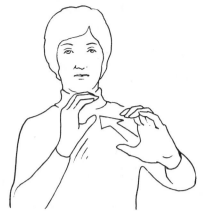

398
initial "c" for car and the other hand
shows its length

car

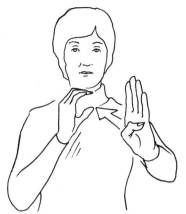

399
initial "B" for bus and the other hand
shows its length.

bus

400
initial "T" for truck and the other
hand shows its length

truck

401
motion of steering

drive

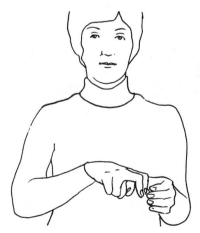

402
passenger sitting in vehicle

ride (inside)

403
wings of plane flying in sky

airplane

bus

car

drive

truck

airplane

ride (inside)

404
boat riding on waves
boat

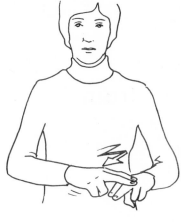

405
refers to railroad tracks
train

406
pedaling a bike
bicycle

407
person riding a horse
ride (straddle)

204

train

boat

ride (straddle)

bicycle

1. The   school   bus   comes   here .

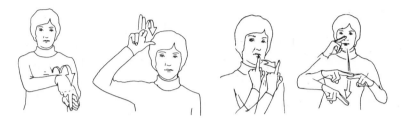

2. Riding   horses   is   fun.

3. The   bicycle   is   red   and   blue.

4. We   will   go   on   the   train.

5. The   car   is   green.

6. Father drove the car home.

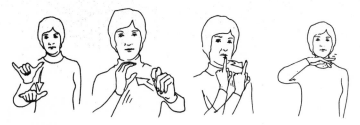

7. The truck is dirty.

8. See the new airplane.

9. We like riding in the car.

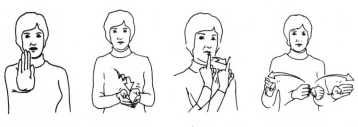

10. Your boat is big.

PRACTICE MAKES PERFECT

15

Watch where you are going.

Your shirt is dirty.

The boy got a haircut.

Lunch time, line up children.

The boy hates school.

He is fighting with my brother.

The children had cake and pop at the party.

We made some popcorn.

The moon comes out at night.

I go to school in the afternoon.

The sun will come out today.

The old dog is hurt.

The fish are swimming in the water.

Please give me the bowl.

I got a toy train for Christmas.

Mother is using the telephone.

Give me the scissors, please.

The turtle moves slowly.

The turkey is for Christmas dinner.

The truck is at the store.

Look at the pretty flowers.

I can't zip up my coat.

We will look at the pictures in the story book.

The hospital helps sick people.

The nurse gives me the medicine.

My sister is writing letters to her friends.

Eat your ice cream.

Pour the coffee.

Drink your milk.

Cut the orange.

I like apple pie.

I want a sandwich and soup, please.

The fire is hot.

Go and get your coat.

The brown boots are mine.

My mother has a pink sweater.

Where are your shoes?

The policeman's shirt is blue.

You will go to the dentist today.

Where is your brother?

What is your friend's name?

The baby is ill.

The children talked to Santa Claus.

The boy has my toy.

You have a dirty face.

The children work in school.

Be quiet, your baby sister is sleeping.

Do you eat potatoes at lunch?

Different foods help you to grow big and strong.

The television is broken.

You can play with your friends today.

The cookies smell good.

Birthday parties are fun.

I will work on the farm.

The hamburger and coke tasted good.

She helped us understand how to use the workboo...

Many animals run and jump.

My friend has glasses and a hearing aid.

The doctor drives a purple car.

Father's chair is broken.

Please give me eight blankets.

It looks like rain; you must close the windows.

Can you catch the ball?

Father opened the door for mother.

I can eat with a fork.

Our flag is red, white and blue.

Your sister is using my pink crayon.

Horses can run fast.

The rabbit is white.

I can write with a pencil.

I finished my work.

Your red shoes are new.

I like ice cream with apple pie.

I ate an orange for breakfast.

Please write your name for me.

Father is reading a book.

My brother climbed a big tree.

The hot tea tasted good.

Children like bananas on ice cream.

Our family is staying home for your birthday party.

Your shoes are in the box.

I like your black boots.

Go to the toilet.

Dry your face and neck.

Monkeys play in the trees.

Mother is cutting some flowers.

Come and take the dog for a walk.

The cat is playing with the mouse.

The cow gives us milk.

Put on your green sweater.

Mother made some cookies today.

You can use my comb.

Please tell me the time.

At breakfast we had bacon and eggs.

Banana cake is good.

Are you hungry?

I like your yellow dress.

The train takes people to town.

Father works out in the sun all day.

You have a letter.

We will go to church tomorrow.

I am mad at you.

Try to finish your work.

The policeman will help you.

Are you happy?

The bad boy hurt the little dog.

Can you throw the ball to me?

Time for your bath.

See the big, black bear.

Be careful, you will fall.

Please bring me the morning paper.

Am I in the right place?

The dentist cleans our teeth.

I will separate the different colored papers for you.

My brother shaves in the morning.

Please give me the salt and pepper.

We have the same name.

My sister looks funny in her new dress.

Here comes the school bus.

Please take your toys off the table.

That is hard work.

I want to play all day.

I can smell the hot popcorn.

I heard the airplane going over my head.

Will you go to town with us tomorrow night?

Please mop the floor again.

Hurry, your father is hungry.

Go to the store and buy some candy.

The boy dropped the tray.

Go around the house and pick up your toys.

Will you please bathe the dog today?

She threw the ball under the car.

My sister is afraid to tell the funny story.

Put on your yellow panties.

The little boy is sad.

I sign and talk at the same time to my deaf friend.

Put on your undershorts.

The children want some gum.

Hi! How are you?

Work is hard to find.

The girl is short and thin.

Change the sheets on your bed.

Put on your yellow shorts today.

The boy has six sheep.

The technician is playing with the children.

My father is sorry that he broke the plate.

Stand here and wait for your mother.

I like sugar in my tea.

I am thirsty.

The nurse smiled at me today.

Wash your hands with soap.

Yes, you can buy a toy at the store.

My brother wants some more meat.

The teacher will drive the school bus.

Go to the bathroom and wash your face.

The stomach pain began yesterday.

Use that broom to sweep the floor.

Crackers are good with a bowl of soup.

It is dark at night.

The little bird is hurt.

The teacher is sitting at her desk.

What is the sign for "it doesn't matter?

Animals are not dumb.

My sister was in the hospital for eleven days.

That is my bed.

Rain! We'd better hurry.

Use your blue blanket.

Look at your picture book.

Put on your new red boots.

The candy bowl is full.

What is in the box?

Find a clean bra.

Is your pencil broken?

We had butter on our toast for breakfast.

Father has a brown coat.

Bring your shoes here.

Buy some ice cream with your money.

We made a cake today.

Mother has a new car.

Change places with me.

Our Christmas tree is pretty.

We went for a ride on the elephant train.

Clean the dirty table.

Color the picture with your crayons.

I am cold. Please close the door.

I am sorry you have a cold.

Put your socks on your feet.

Hi! I am happy to see you here.

She learned how to sew in school.

My friend has four little pigs.

No more hot dogs for me, I am full.

I know him, he is my sister's boyfriend.

Where is your knife and spoon?

It is light in the daytime.

Santa Claus is laughing.

How much money can we have today?

Mother has the lights on at night.

Next time you can pay for the dinner.

No one is ugly.

The morning sun is orange.

The nine boys are playing ball.

INDEX

SIGN LANGUAGE
School Supplies

133 LIBRARY SURVIVAL SIGNS
Joyce Media, Inc.

$1.60   CODE: 390

A basic vocabulary of 133 most-used library signs. A must for every school, college, or public library. Ten mini dictionaries to the package. Pocket sized. Eight full pages. Printed on heavy paper.

the American sign language alphabet

SIGN LANGUAGE POSTER (23"x35")
Joyce Media

$2.95   CODE: 240

Giant 23"x35" poster shows the American Sign Language alphabet from A to Z. Clarity sets this poster apart from all others in its class. Easily visible from any desk in a normal size classroom. Printed on very heavy paper stock.

ALPHABET POSTERS - 17"x23"
Joyce Media Inc.

$1.95   CODE: 914

A medium size poster of the American Manual Alphabet. Fits the normal size bulletin board. A wonderful way to expose a hearing classroom to the beauty of American Sign Language.

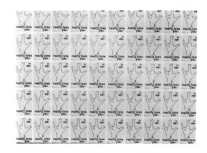

110 SCHOOL SURVIVAL SIGNS
Jay Belcher, Editor

$1.25   CODE: 835

Mini Sign Language dictionary of 110 most-used signs in schools. Ideal for mainstream schools where administrators, staff, nurses, parents, peers, and friends want to know those emergency and social signs basic to communication. Wallet sized. Ten dictionaries to each shrink-wrapped package.

"I REALLY LOVE YOU" STICKERS

$1.25   CODE: 833

Fifty clever, cheery, self-adhesive stickers per sheet. Perfect to brighten up envelopes, packages, boxes, letters, cards, and notes.

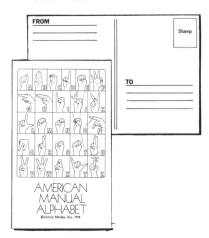

ALPHABET POSTCARD
Joyce Media Inc.

$2.99   CODE: 915

Ten handy postcards for dashing off that quick note, or thoughful remembrance. Ten cents mails any message first class.

SIGN LANGUAGE RUBBER STAMPS
Joyce Media Inc.

$39.95   CODE: 271

Twenty-six individual rubber stamps, one for each letter of the alphabet. Hardwood with rubber cushion. Shows hand sign with corresponding letter. Packaged in clear plastic holding box. Ink pad included.

122 WORK SURVIVAL SIGNS
Joyce Media, Inc.

10/$1.60   CODE: 343

Ten mini dictionaries per package. 122 helpful signs designed to aid communication with hearing impaired persons in a work environment.

MEDICAL SURVIVAL SIGNS
Joyce Media Inc.

$1.25   CODE: 966

A basic vocabulary of 100 most-used medical signs. Colors, numbers, letters, and handsigns for pain, dizzy, drink, breathe, sleepy, x-ray, water, pill, etc. An absolute must for hospitals, paramedic units, doctor's offices, nurse's offices, and medical schools. Ten of these mini dictionaries per package.

SIGN LANGUAGE
School Supplies

PANCOM
California School for the Deaf, Riverside

PANCOM represents an investment of $100,000, and two years of research to produce a complete, self contained learning module for parents and staff beginning total communication. The picture books and the sound, color cassettes match precisely. The unit was designed to be circulated from house to house and classroom to classroom so that parents, teachers, children, and staff can have the same basic sign vocabulary to begin from. Ideal for media centers to loan out.

PANCOM - FAIRCHILD CARTREEL PROJECTOR
Fairchild Camera Co.

$550   CODE: 326

Fairchild Model 900 cartreel projector. Forward, Reverse, Stop Action, Sound.

PANCOM-LEVEL 1 FILM CASSETTES
California School for the Deaf-Riverside
$975   CODE: 327

PANCOM-LEVEL 2 FILM CASSETTES
California School for the Deaf-Riverside
$1290   CODE: 328

PANCOM - PICTURE MANUAL LEVEL 1
California School for the Deaf-Riverside
$9.95   CODE: 324

PANCOM - PICTURE MANUAL LEVEL 2
California School for the Deaf-Riverside
$12.95   CODE: 325

PANCOM - PROJECTOR SHIPPING CASE
California School for the Deaf-Riverside
$220   CODE: 330

PANCOM - FILM SHIPPING CASE
California School for the Deaf-Riverside
$280   CODE: 329

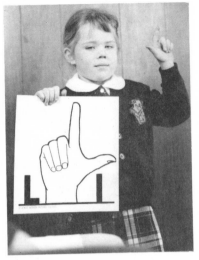

ALPHABET WALL CARDS
Joyce Media Inc.

$9.95   CODE: 344

Large and clear. Each card measures 11"x12." Sharp black on white. Easily visible from any place in an average size classroom. Twenty-six cards in all. One card for every letter of the alphabet.

"SIGN LANGUAGE USED HERE!" SIGN
Joyce Media Inc.

$0.90   CODE: 858

These self adhesive signs alert signing persons that sign language may be used to communicate. Measures 4"x5" Makes people feel welcome.

I LOVE YOU - SELF INKING - X STAMPER
Joyce Media

$7.95   CODE: 999

Handy, self inking stamper to correct papers, customize notes, etc. Good for 50,000 impressions and then it can be re-inked. Available in red ink only.

PENCIL "I LOVE YOU" STAMPER
Joyce Media Inc.

$5.95   CODE: 998

Pre-inked "I Love You" pencil cap stamp gives up to 50,000 impressions without re-inking, but may be re-inked at any time. Comes with protective cover. 11/16" diameter. Available in red ink only. Perfect for correcting papers.

SIGN LANGUAGE
Louie J. Fant

$12.95   CODE: 159

Sign language is the fourth most-use language in America today, according several recent estimates. This beginni book features outstandingly sha photography along with Louie Fan easy and conversational style. This is t Sign Language textbook used at CSU (Cal. State Northridge) and at ma other locations around the country. teaches sign language the way the v majority of adult deaf persons commu cate.

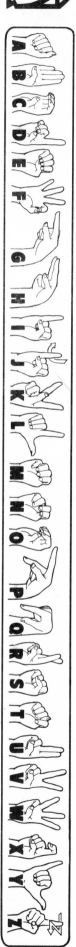

AMESLAN - AN INTRODUCTION TO AMERICAN SIGN LANGUAGE
Louie J. Fant

$6.95   CODE: 21

The most widely used textbook of Ameslan (ASL or American Sign Language) in the world today. Written by Louie J. Fant, Jr., whose parents were both deaf. This author learned sign language as his "mother tongue." His basic conversational approach makes learning sign language a very fun and enjoyable experience.

WARD'S NATURAL SIGN LANGUAGE THESAURUS OF USEFUL SIGNS AND SYNONYMS
Jill Ward

$19.95   CODE: 446

Thesaurus (thi-sor-es) comes from a Greek word which means treasure or collection. This is the first such book ever produced. Already in its second printing after only four months. Over 2500 clear, concise photographs of signs and their synonyms. Particularly helpful for showing how one sign can mean many different concepts. An absolutely essential reference book for every parent, teacher, administrator, or library.

SIGN LANGUAGE FOR EVERYONE
California State Dept. of Health

$12.95   CODE: 134

This text is an excellent basic book for beginning signers who wish to learn Signed English and the Total Communication Method of Sign Language. Each sign is shown with its English word meaning underneath and at the end of each chapter there are complete practice sentences with the signs printed above each word. For added practice, each sign drawing has the English meaning printed on the reverse page so that the whole book can be used as flash cards.

AMESLAN AUDIO CASSETTES
Louie J. Fant

$34.95   CODE: 46

15 half-hour presentations let the beginning signer hear Louie J. Fant explain each chapter in the Ameslan Sign Language textbook. Mr. Fant explains each sign and sentence throughout the book. He encourages, helps, shares vital insights into what it means to be deaf, to be a hearing son of deaf parents and what good a skilled signer can accomplish today. These tapes were designed for hearing people who want excellent individual study. Many teachers play these tapes to their sign language classes and then observe each student's grasp and skill.

PLAY IT BY SIGN
Suzie Linton Kirchner

$12.95   CODE: 16

For adults or children learning manual communication and fun for anybody who already knows sign language. Some of the games may also be used for children or adults who are autistic, aphasic, brain damaged, mentally retarded, deaf/blind, or exceptionally gifted. Twenty-six games in all. Bound in a one inch, three ring, heavy duty vinyl binder so that game pages may be easily removed to teach from, copy, or add to. Personal notes, additional pages, reminders, etc., may be easily inserted on 8½x11 sheets.

LEISURE TIME ACTIVITIES FOR DEAF-BLIND CHILDREN
Mikalonis and Huffman

$12.95   CODE: 31

Ninety-four activities presented in this manual are meant for parents, foster parents, aunts, uncles, brothers, sisters, teachers, and friends of deaf-blind children. Four California state hospitals (Fairview, Pacific, Poterville, and Sonoma) had deaf-blind projects which were cooperatively funded by the California State Department of Health and the Southwest Region Deaf-Blind Center.

SIGN LANGUAGE
School Supplies

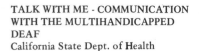

SIGNS FOR ALL SEASONS
Suzie Linton Kirchner

$12.95   CODE: 149

Contains 50 games and activities to be played in pantomime, gestures, finger-spelling, and sign language. The games and activities can be used for initial teaching, as reinforcement for previously learned material, or just for fun. They are meant not only for hearing impaired children and adults, but also for others with normal hearing whose minds are language locked, rather than their ears.

American Sign
Language Alphabet

MANUAL ALPHABET CARDS
Joyce Media Inc.

$5.95   CODE: 919

One hundred cards per package. Wallet sized. Shows the American Manual Alphabet on the front and hand signs for numbers from one to ten. Printed on light cardboard.

NOTEBOOK SIZE MANUAL ALPHABET PAGES - A
Joyce Media Inc.

10 for $1.50   CODE: 912

These convenient 8½"x11" notebook pages come in packages of ten and show the American Manual Alphabet in a clear, clever, cartoon way. For classroom reward or as a unit on sign language. Ten pages per package. Three hole punched.

NOTEBOOK SIZE MANUAL ALPHABET PAGES - B
Joyce Media Inc.

10 for $1.50   CODE: 913

An exact, small duplicate of our famous large poster. Handy for notebooks. Three hole punched. Ten pages per package. Ideal for sign language classes or to pass out to hearing classroom with a desire to learn about sign language.

HAZARDS OF DEAFNESS
Roy K. Holcomb

$8.95   CODE: 457

The more than 700 "HAZARDS" which follow give the reader a keen insight into the world of silence. It also shows that all deaf people are alike - and different - in their experiences. With these hazards so vividly exemplified by Mr. Holcomb, the deaf people have assessed their assets and liabilities and, with these experiences being shared with others, they see empathy coming out of you.

> "The hearing must see what the deaf experience is, if they are to know and understand us thoroughly."
> Edward E. Corbett, Jr.

GESTURES
Dorothy Miles

$6.95   CODE: 175

Dorothy Miles is the most advanced and best known poet alive today. This compact volume of her 39 latest poems speaks eloquently for herself and the whole changing world of the hearing impaired. Many of the poems were written expressly to be performed in the language of the signs.

TALK WITH ME - COMMUNICATION WITH THE MULTIHANDICAPPED DEAF
California State Dept. of Health

$14.95   CODE: 29

The Deaf Task Force of the California State Department of Health standardized this 400 sign vocabulary by carefully analyzing all existing sign language textbooks and choosing which signs would be the most useful, understandable and manageable for multihandicapped deaf persons in state hospitals. Each sign is drawn large and clear with its English name and meaning printed underneath. On the back of each sign is printed the English word so that each page can be used as flash cards. There is an extensive collection of learning activities to reinforce the signs. This text has proven useful with autistic, aphasic, brain damaged, mentally retarded, slow learners, TMR and others.

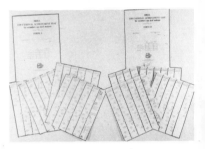

BRILL EDUCATIONAL ACHIEVEMENT TEST FOR SECONDARY AGE DEAF STUDENTS
Richard G. Brill, Ed.D.

FORM A: C-561
FORM B: C-563
$1.25

Score Key AC-562
Score Key BC-564
$12.95

STANDARDIZATION PROCESS
This test was standardized on 1,010 prelingual deaf subjects covering the chronological age range of 15 through 18 inclusive. The subject areas of the four subtests are common subjects for pupils of secondary age. The original questions were pretested and analyzed by administering them to 300 pupils in three schools for the deaf in California. After analyzing the results, Forms A and B were developed as parallel forms. The tests were administered to approximately 1,010 pupils in 29 schools for the deaf throughout the United States. The scores from this national sample of students form the basis of the norms. The Conversion Table is based on the total sample and thus an individual's percentile or standard score shows his standing relative to other deaf secondary age students in the United States.